BODIE

Images From a California Ghost Town Suspended in Time

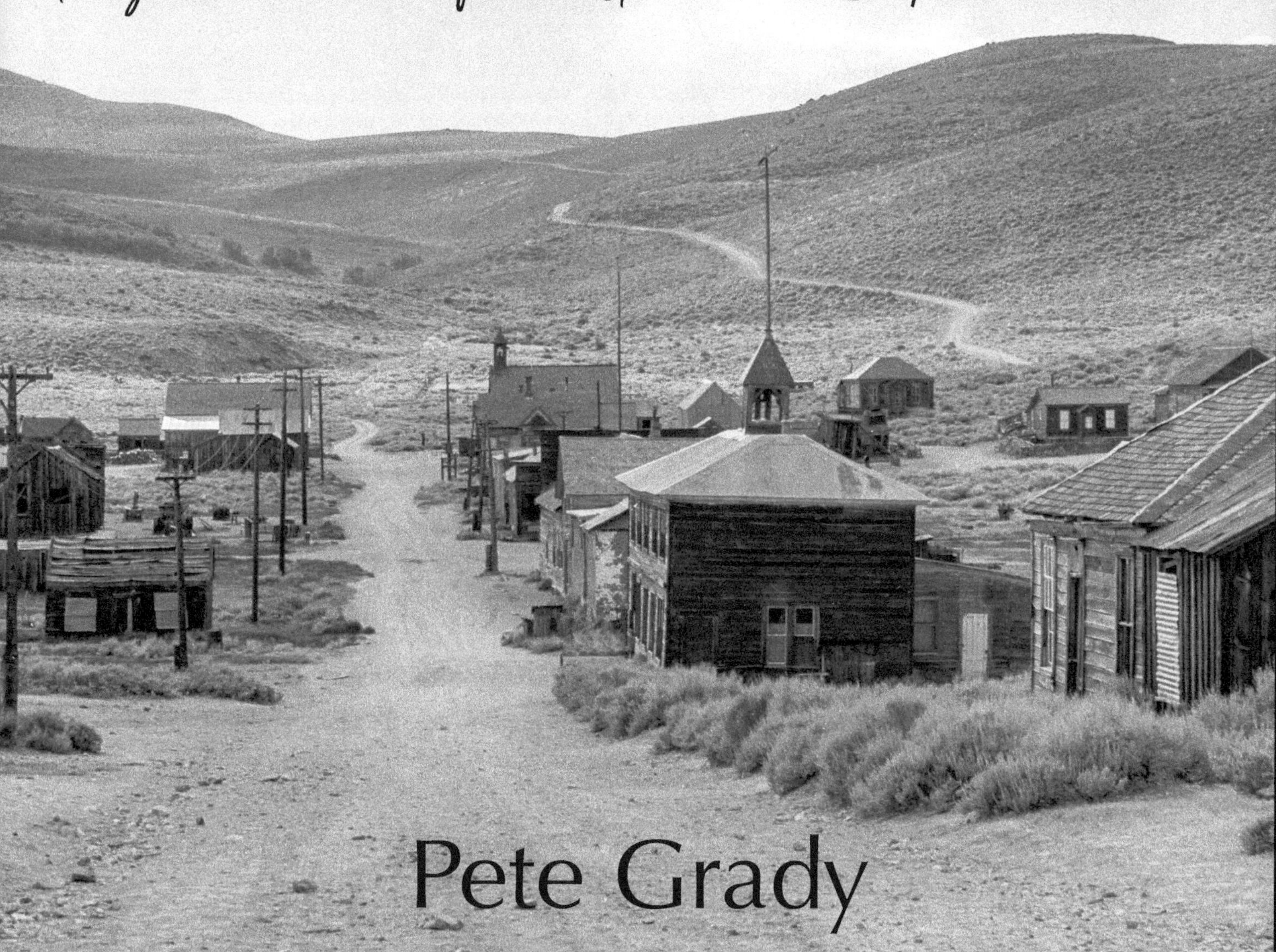

Pete Grady

BODIE

Images From a California Ghost Town Suspended in Time

Hardcover ISBN: 978-1-61206-228-0
Softcover ISBN: 978-0-9762642-1-7

Photography by: Pete Grady
Project Management by: Heather Goetter
Graphic Design by: Fusion Creative Works, FusionCW.com

Published by

AlohaPublishing.com

Printed in the United States of America

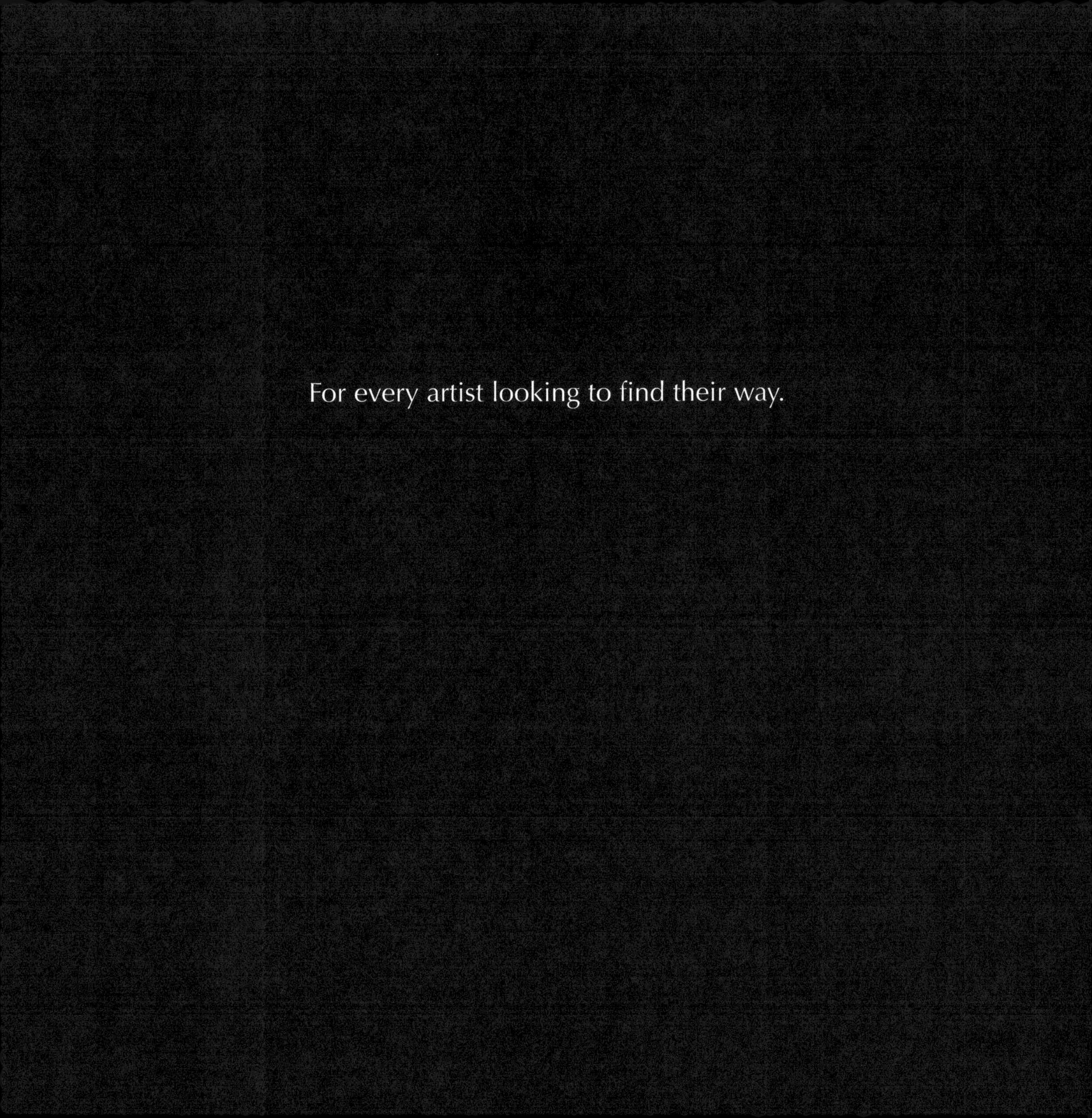

For every artist looking to find their way.

Why I Wrote This Book

By virtue of its stunningly austere setting and intact and unspoiled condition, Bodie emits a sort of gravity that attracts Wild West enthusiasts, history buffs, road trippers, and ghost town aficionados. Over a half century ago, California's State Park system took on the responsibility of protecting, maintaining, and interpreting this remarkable cultural artifact and opens Bodie to visitors daily as weather permits. Limited mostly to exploring the exteriors of its buildings and the surrounding terrain, a small museum and a guided tour of the stamp mill are the only accessible interior spaces in the park. I had been to Bodie twice and was familiar with the starkly rugged character of its buildings and the assorted clutter of tools, implements, and shells of automobiles strewn about the landscape. It is easy to see and feel the nostalgic character of this gold rush town, to absorb the romantic sentimentality bolstered by the collection of visual cues that have informed our notions about the era in which Bodie flourished. Gazing through the windows from sidewalks and porches, I longed for a chance to explore the interiors and examine the treasures within.

Eventually I found myself with just that opportunity. A group of photographers had been assembled and permissions had been sought to gain entry to a few of the more interesting structures. I eagerly accepted an invitation to be part of that group. Plans were formulated, equipment and materials agreed on, and we waited for the date with great anticipation. Diverting east from Highway 395 into the foothills of the Sierra Nevada Mountains' eastern edge, Bodie is the terminus of a half hour of twists and turns, the last three miles of it on washboarded dirt. We converged in several vehicles and were greeted by rangers and given an orientation. Satisfied that we knew the rules and expectations we split up, following them to one of several buildings.

As I entered the buildings, a transformation began to take place. The crisp, almost harsh light outside gave way to a soft, enveloping glow that reached every corner. A fine layer of dust coated the walls, floors and every object, simplifying the forms and enhancing the light's revealing quality. I was struck by the arbitrariness of how the objects had been abandoned, as if the occupants had gotten a call to leave, rose up that very moment, and vanished. What remained, for me, was a Pompeii-like tableau of everyday life, a frozen moment that transcended Bodie's sentimentalized reputation. Objects lost much of their intrinsic sense of purpose, becoming more abstract and sculptural. I came to see Bodie in a much different way, inside and out. Repairs and additions on buildings took on new meaning—the impulse and intentions were completely utilitarian yet culminated in strangely artful vignettes, when selected and framed in the right way through my camera.

What is offered here are images with intimacy and universality, affirmed by the happenstance arrangements of objects both familiar and curious, and detached from the Wild West character of Bodie that has made its way into our psyche. It is my hope to reveal the previously unspoken testimony of this town as a proxy for dreams anticipated, persisted in, and forgotten.

Pete Grady

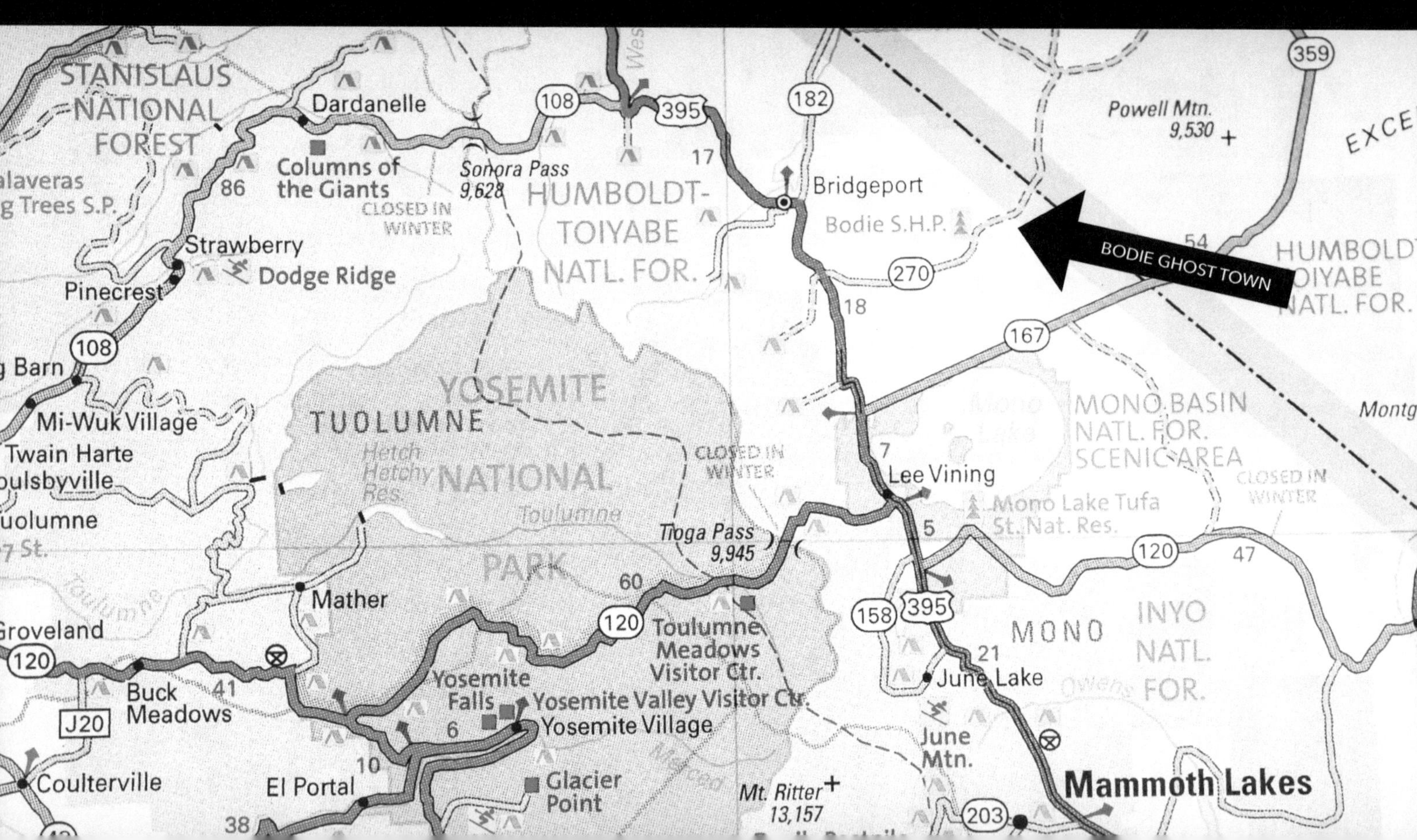

Bodie State Park, California

This Californian ghost town began as a small mining camp in 1859. William "Waterman" Bodie, this town's namesake, discovered gold in the hills southeast of Lake Tahoe, California, but died in a blizzard the following year.

Less than 20 years later, a huge deposit of gold-rich ore was discovered in the area and almost overnight, Bodie became a Wild West boomtown. At its peak, almost 10,000 people lived, worked, and flourished in Bodie. There were around 2,000 buildings, including banks, multiple fire companies, newspapers, a jail, a mortuary, schools, and churches. This Wild West town also had the expected "businesses of ill repute," including 65 saloons, multiple brothels, as well as gambling halls, and opium dens.

At the height of its boom, the mix of gold, money, and alcohol often had fatal results. Newspapers reported that townspeople would regularly inquire in the morning, "Have we a man for breakfast?" Which was their way of asking if anyone had died the night before.

Bodie's slow decline began in 1880 when the single, gold-hungry men were lured away to gold-rich areas like Butte, Montana, and Tombstone, Arizona. Families held on as long as possible, but eventually moved away, one by one.

By 1910, the population of this once bustling town was down to 698. Bodie is now a ghost town.

In 1961, California declared it the official state gold rush ghost town and it became a historic landmark.

Today visitors can walk down the deserted streets and peer in the windows of the 110 remaining structures to see glimpses of the past in a state of "arrested decay."

https://www.bodie.com

https://www.visitmammoth.com/blogs/history-and-geology-bodie-ghost-town

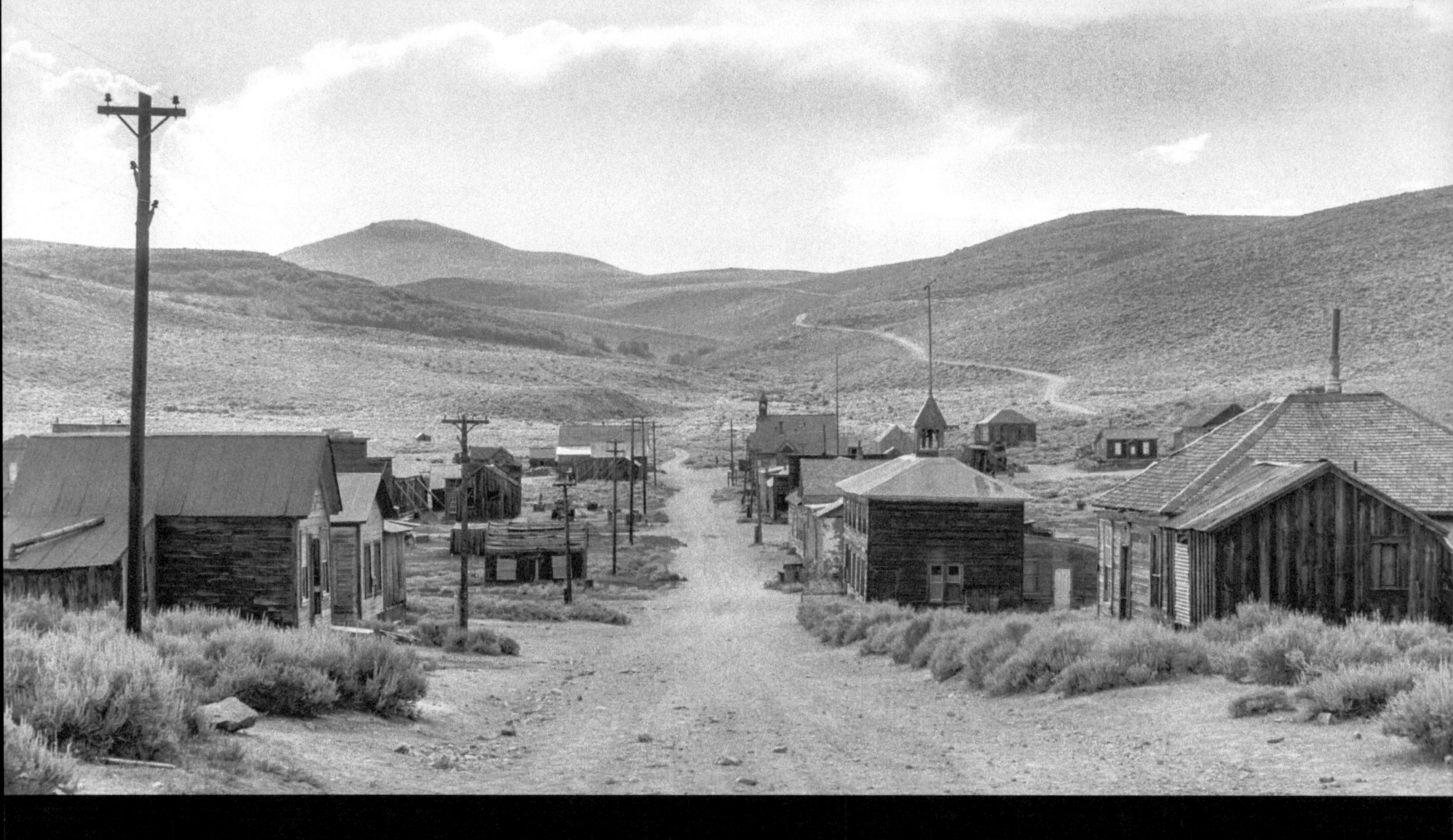

The road from nowhere. Looking west down Green St. from the Wood St. intersection,

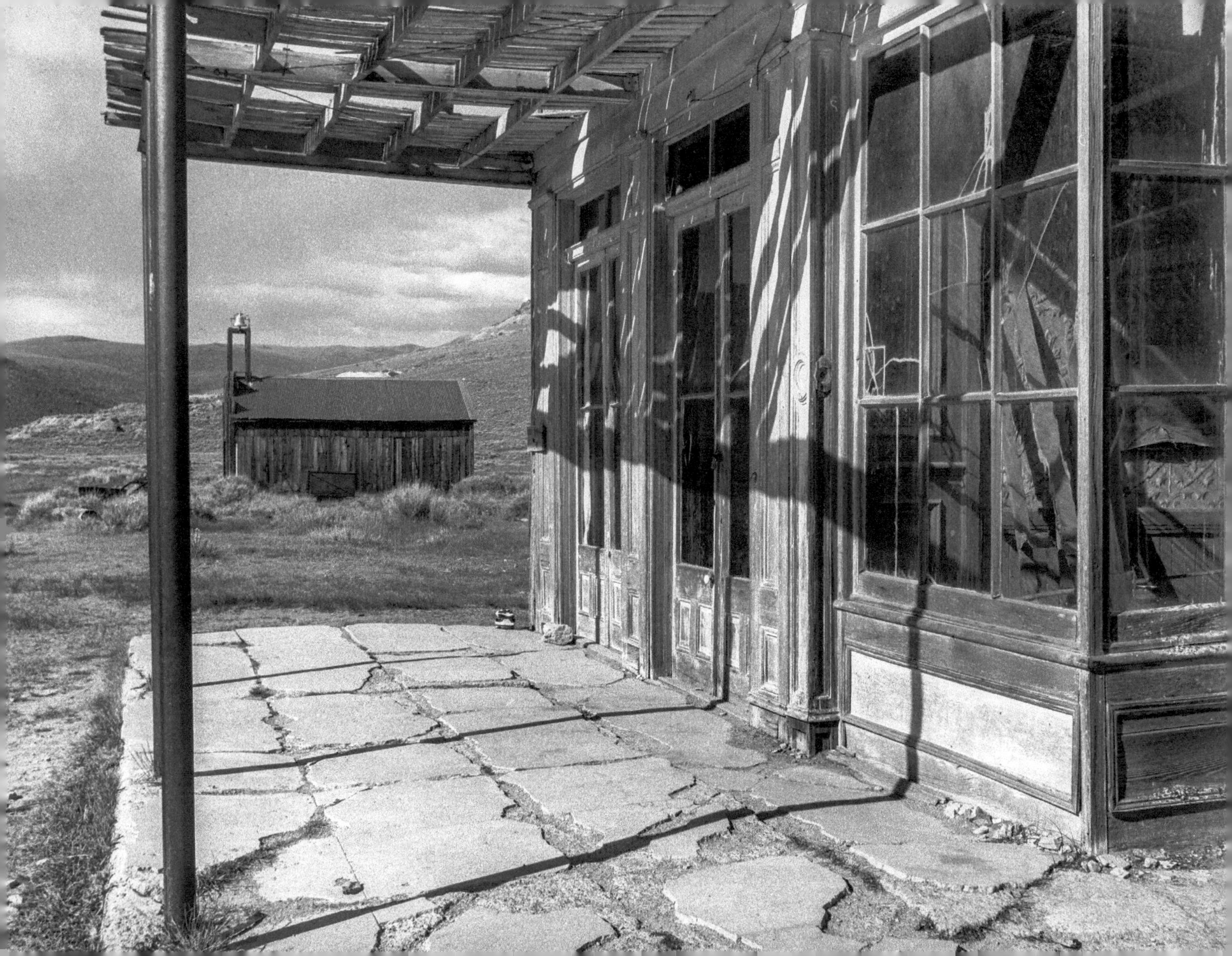

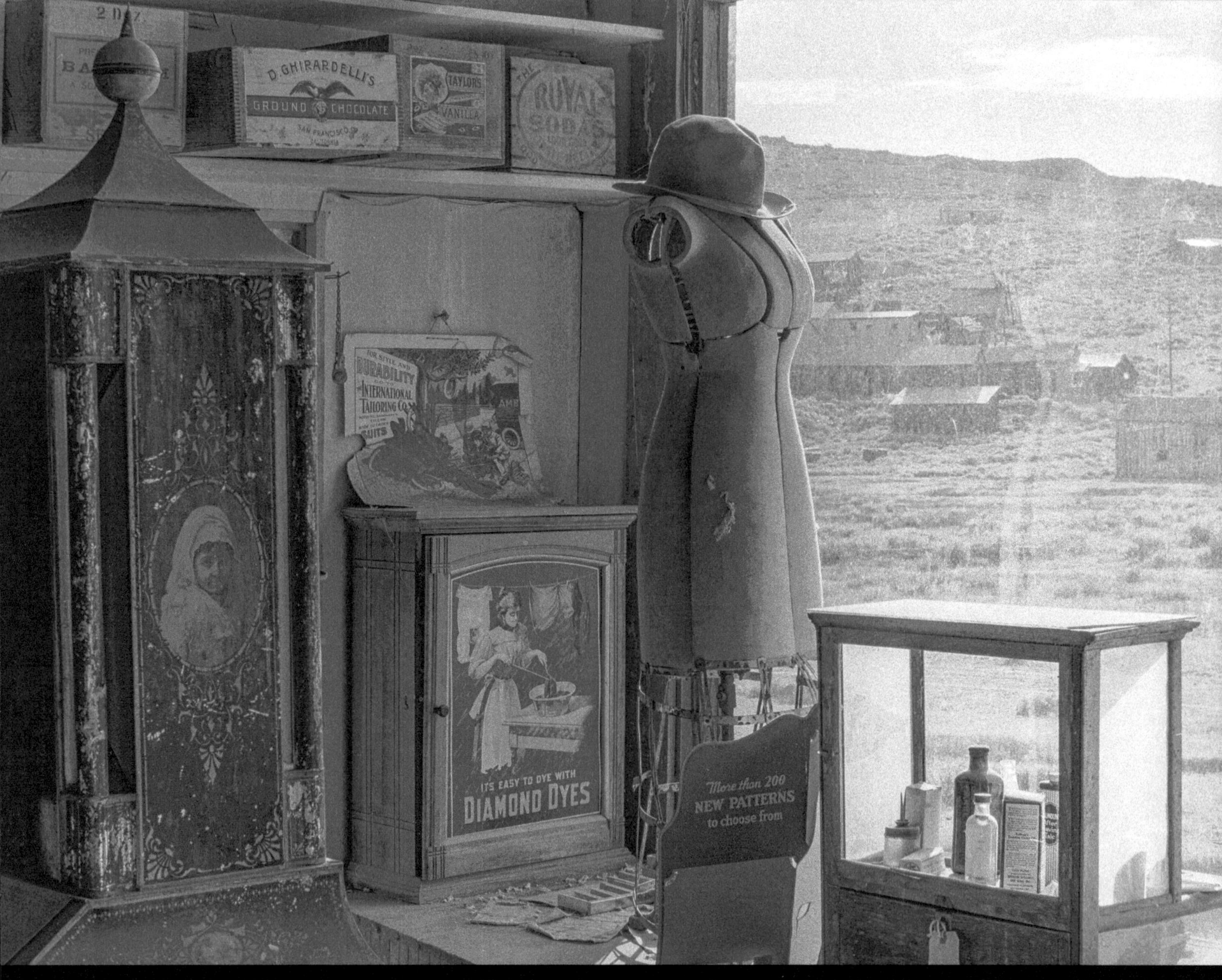

A hatted dress form gazes out from the general store toward the Standard Mill.

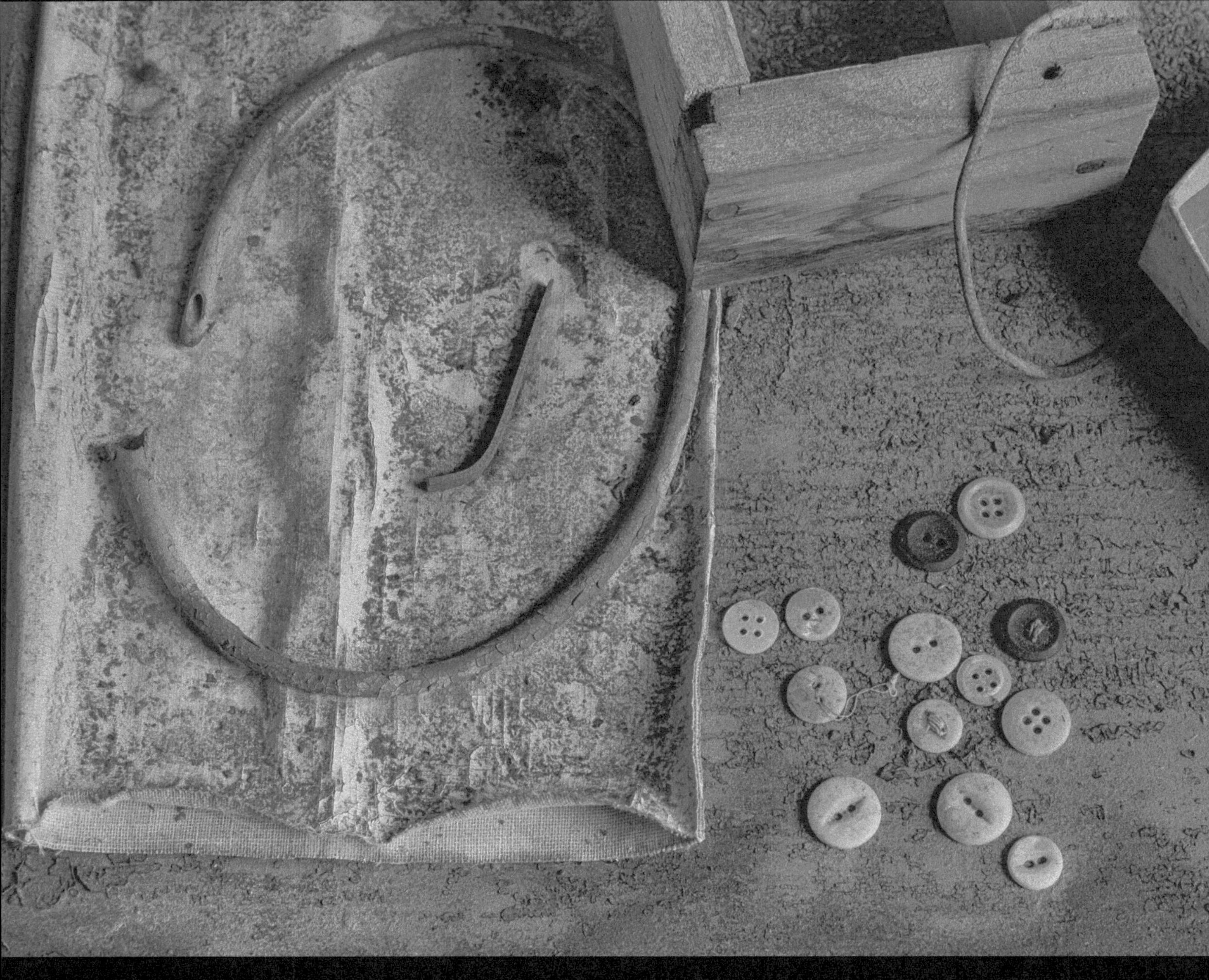

A little of this and a little of that. The general store provided practical things like buttons and a variety of curious oddments.

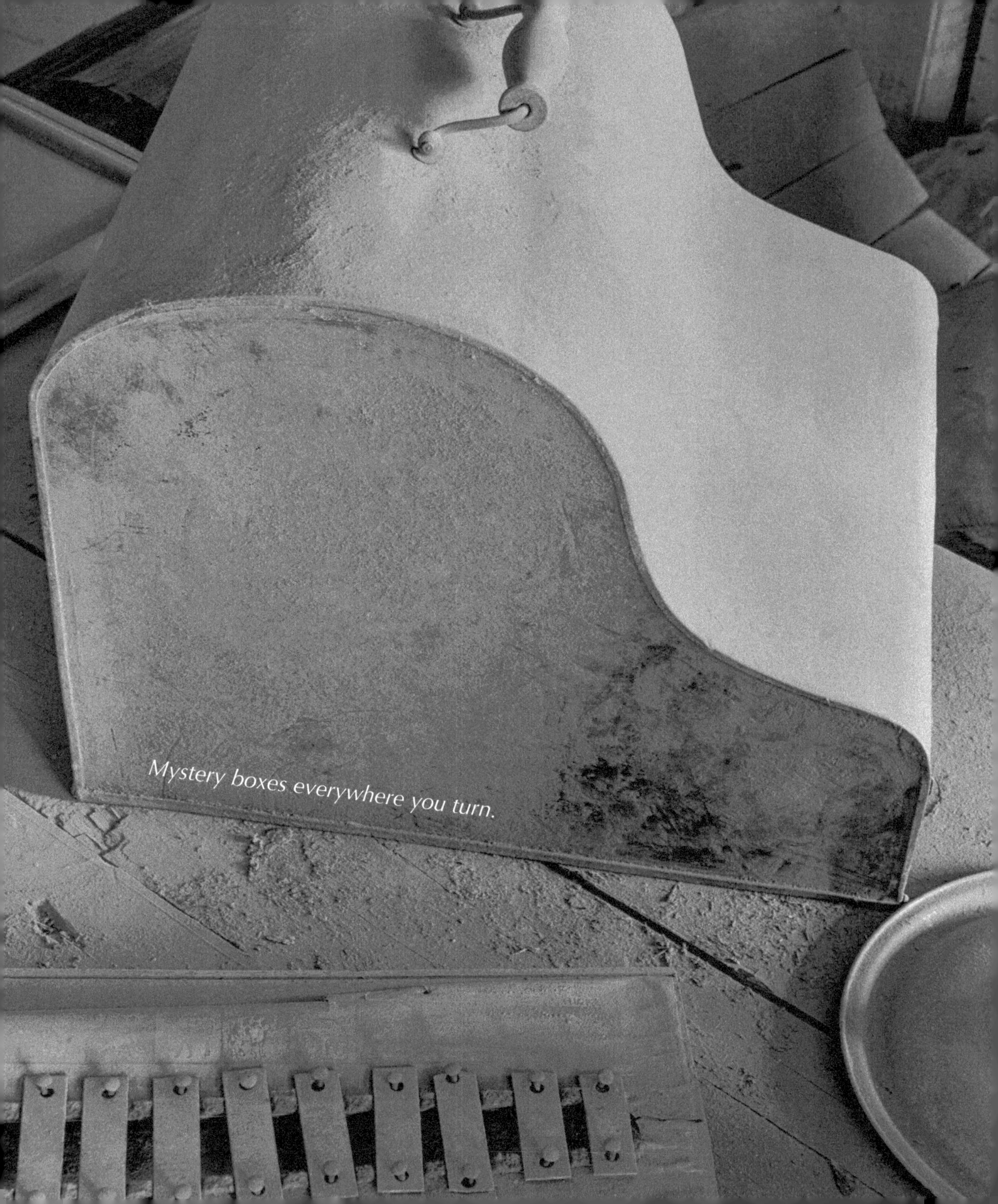

Mystery boxes everywhere you turn.

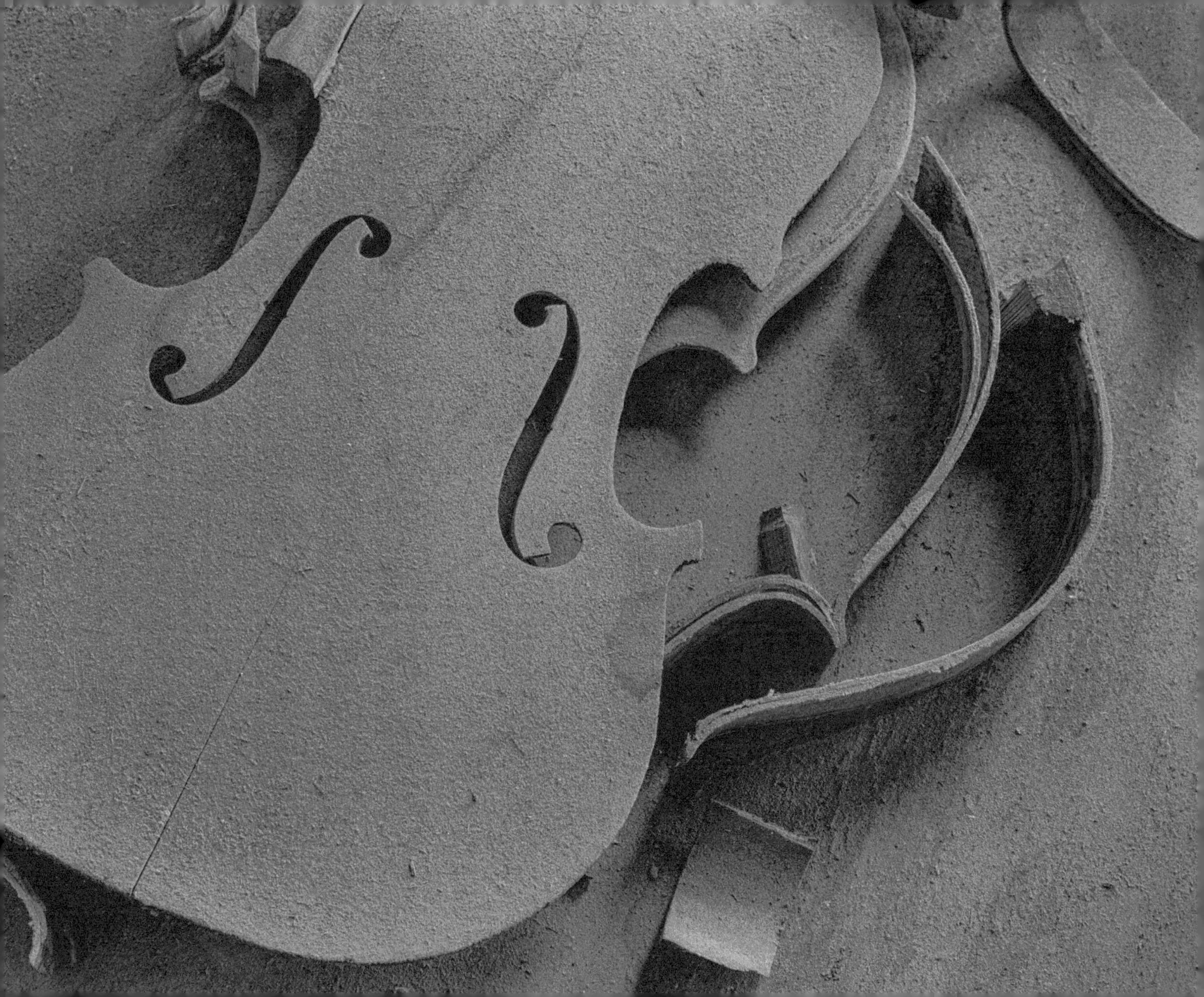

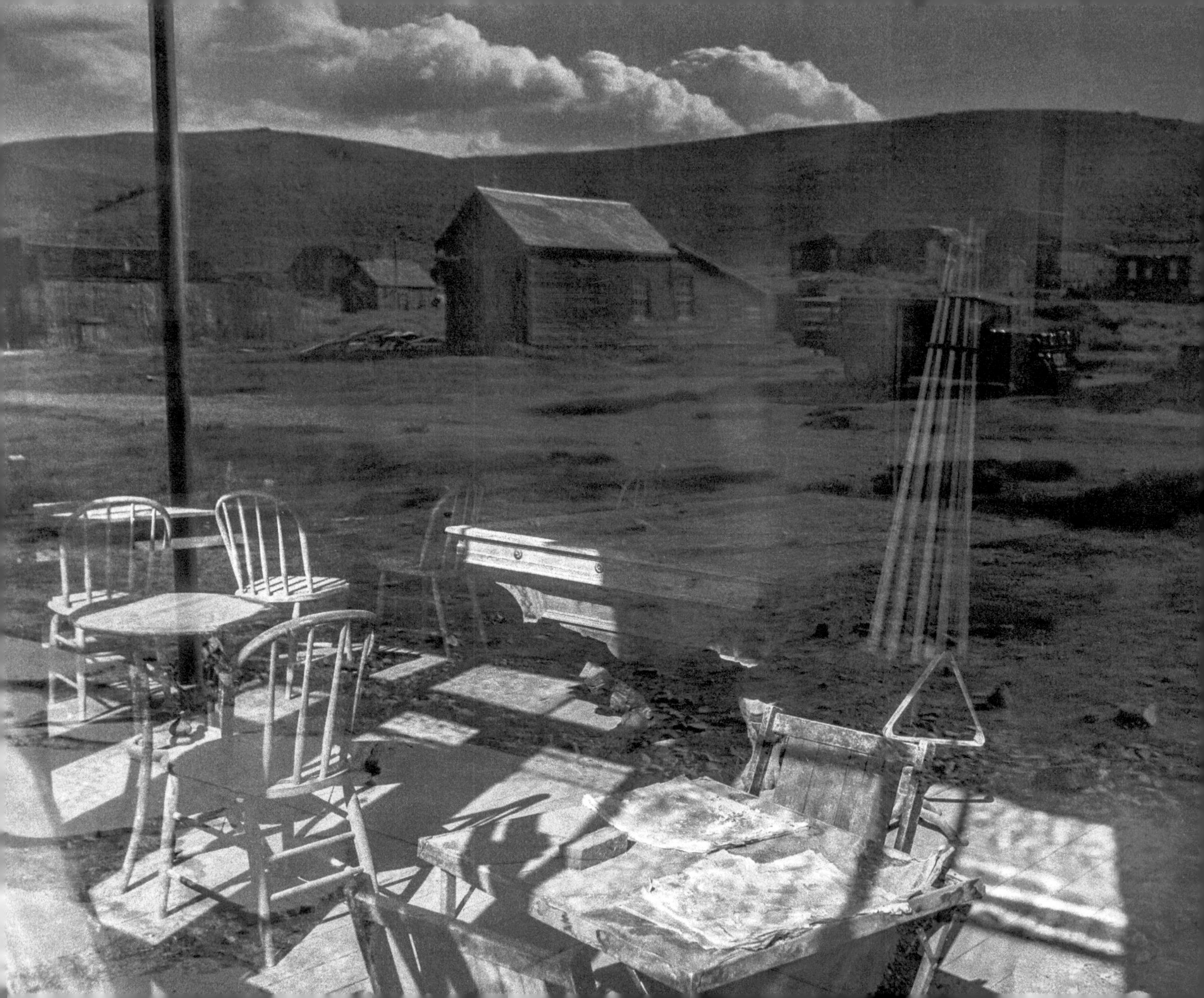

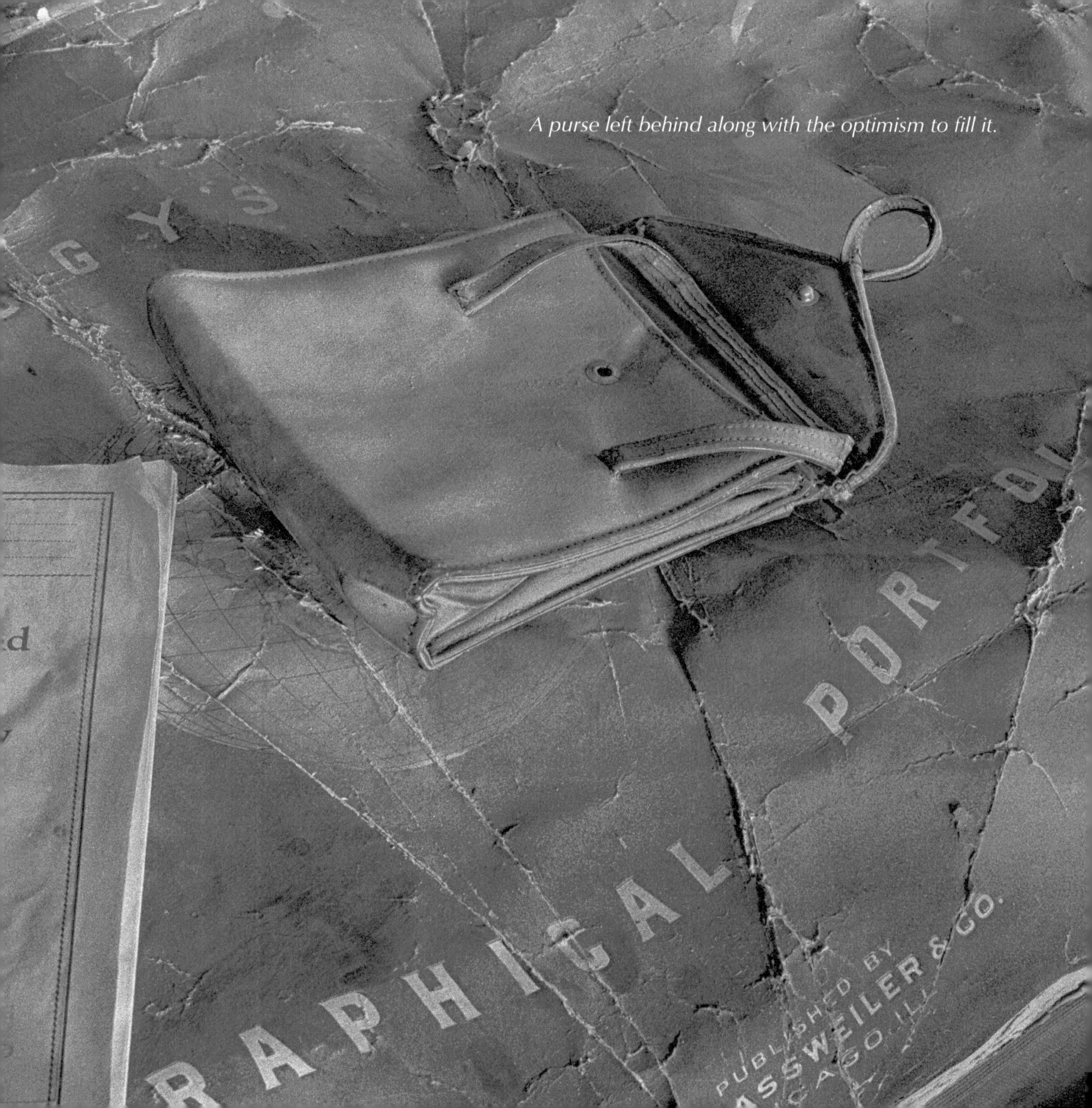

A purse left behind along with the optimism to fill it.

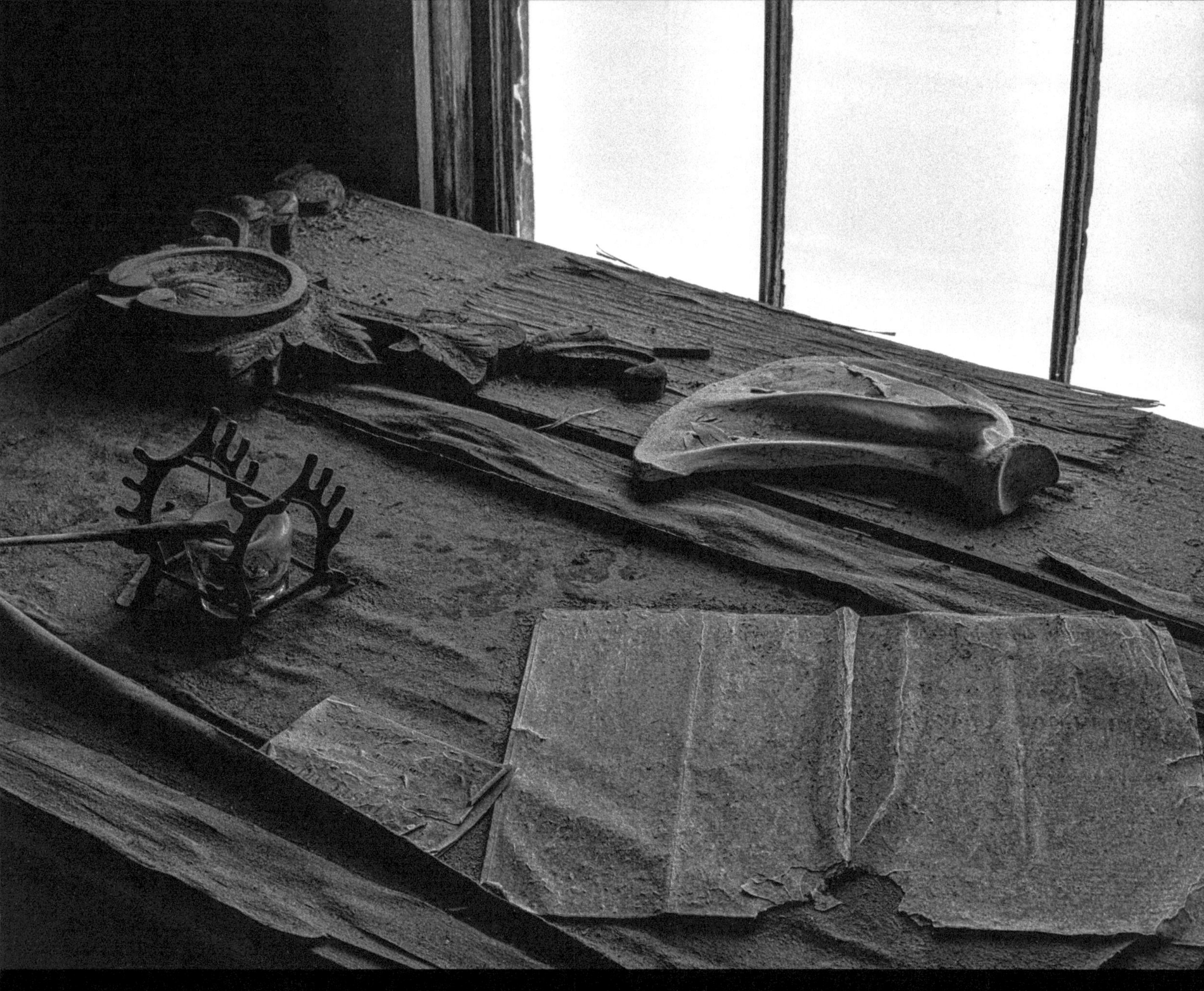

The hazy glow of Bodie's windows envelop both common and curious artifacts.

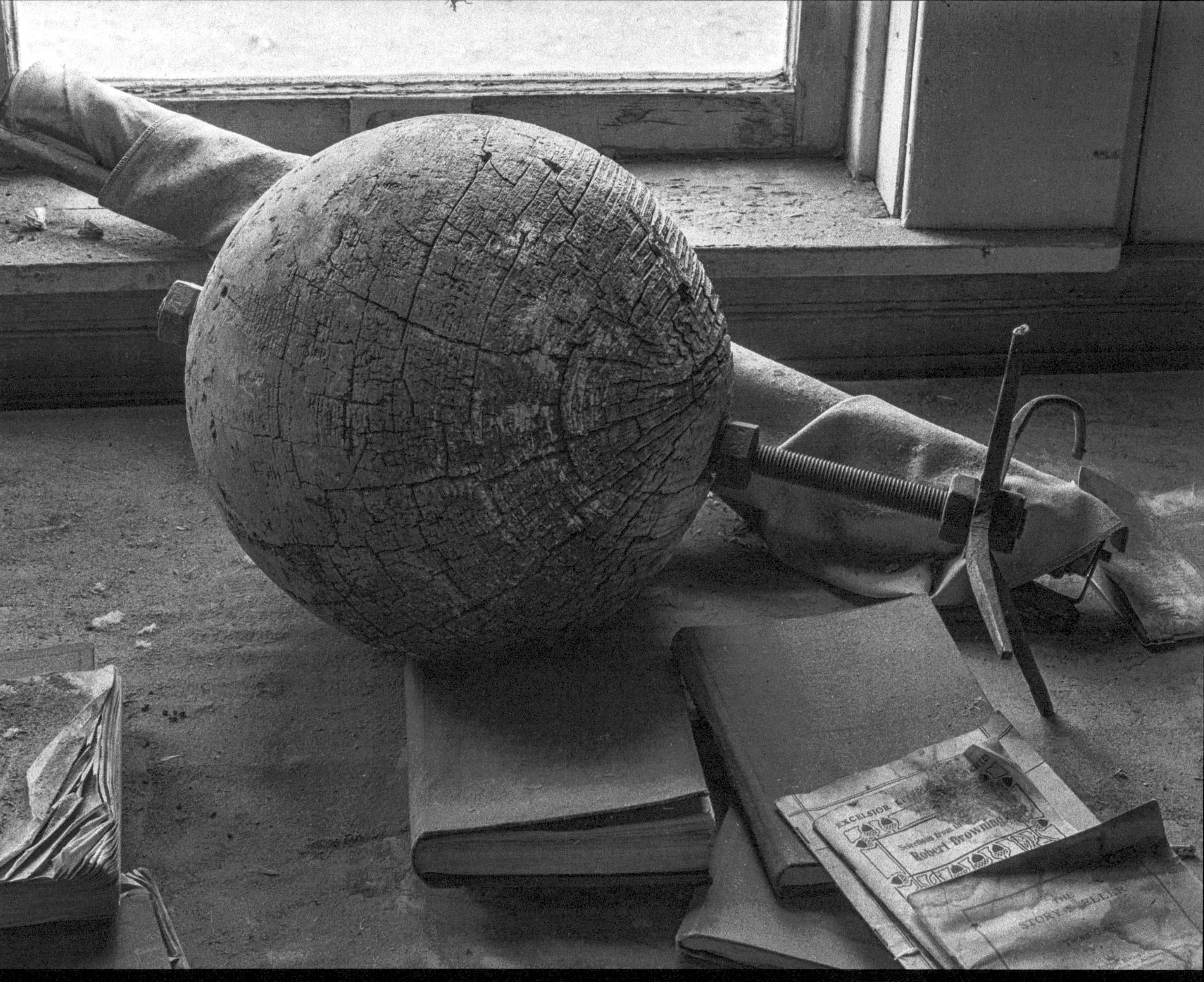

A classroom globe attests to the desiccating harshness of the Bodie climate.
The result is part fascination, part prophesy.

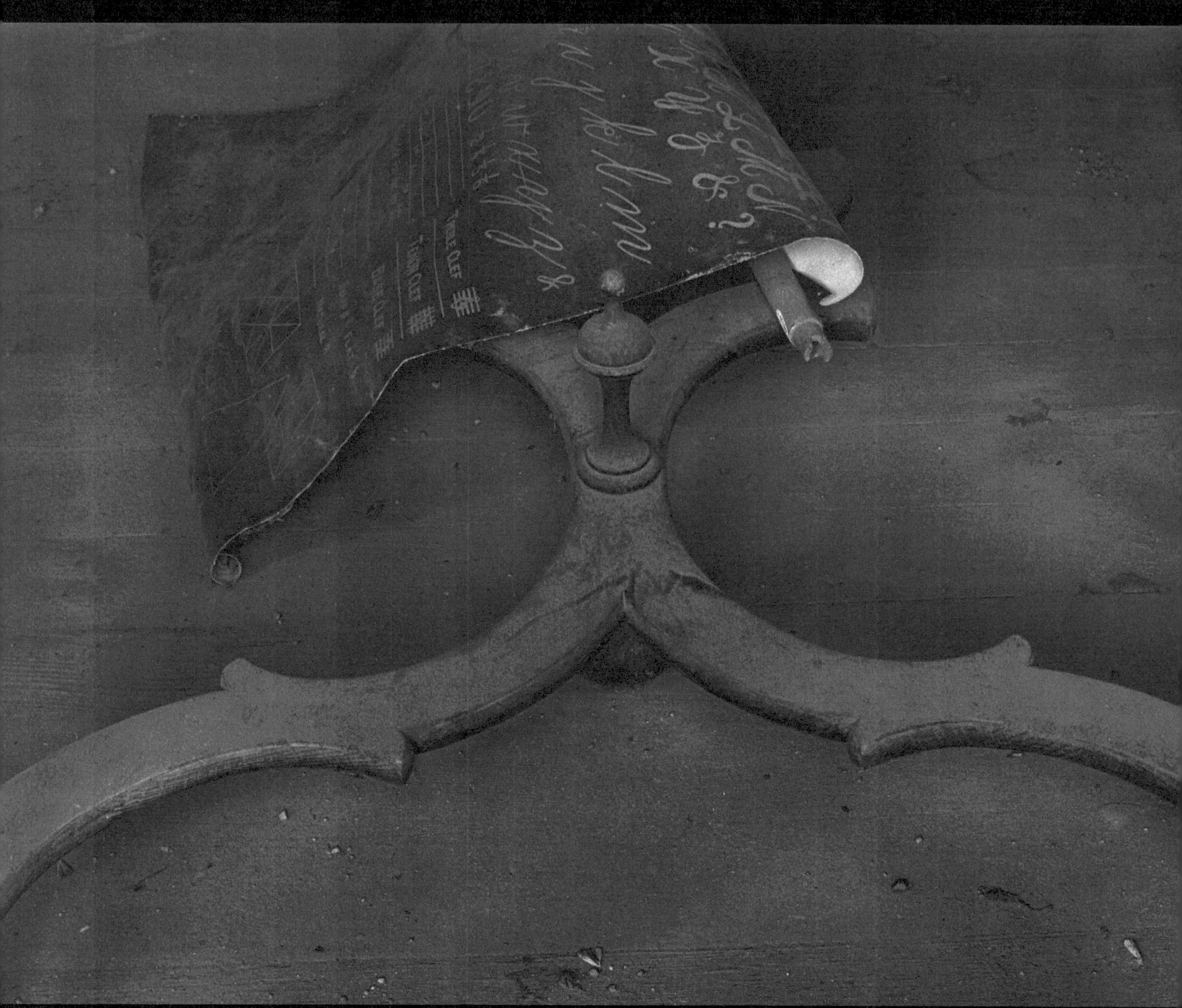

The arabesque stretcher of a library table mirrors the cursive forms on a handwriting chart.

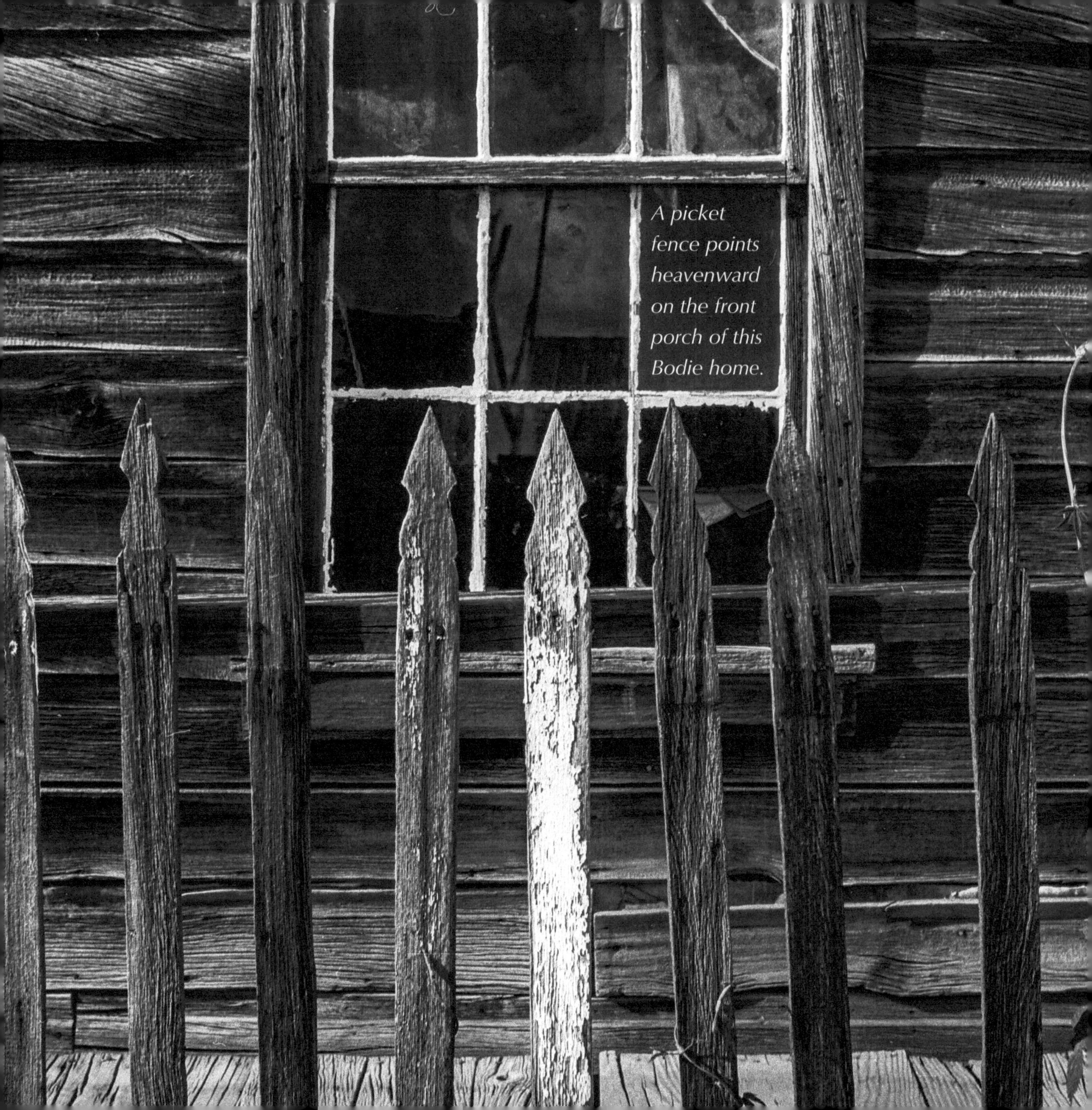

A picket fence points heavenward on the front porch of this Bodie home.

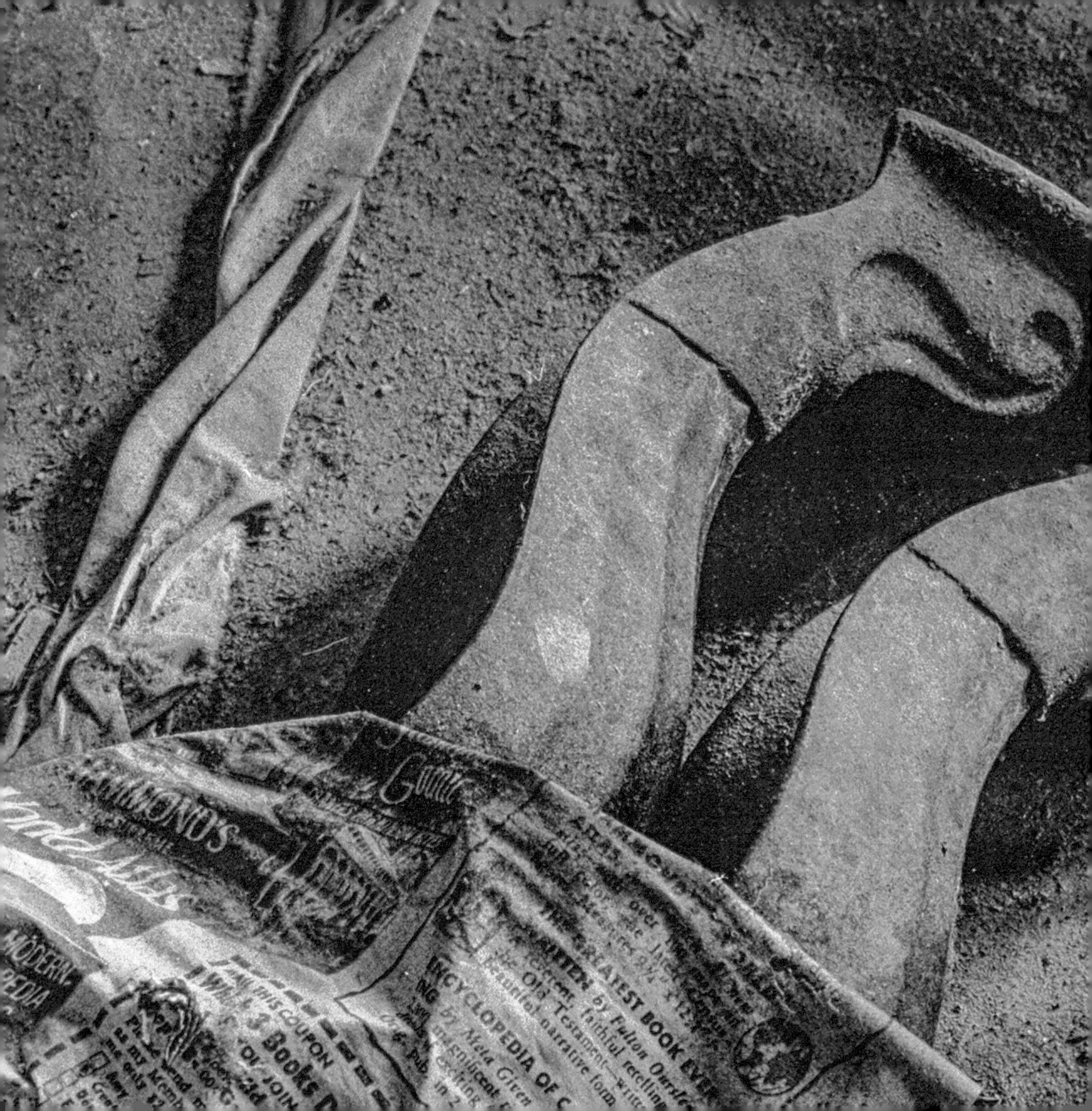

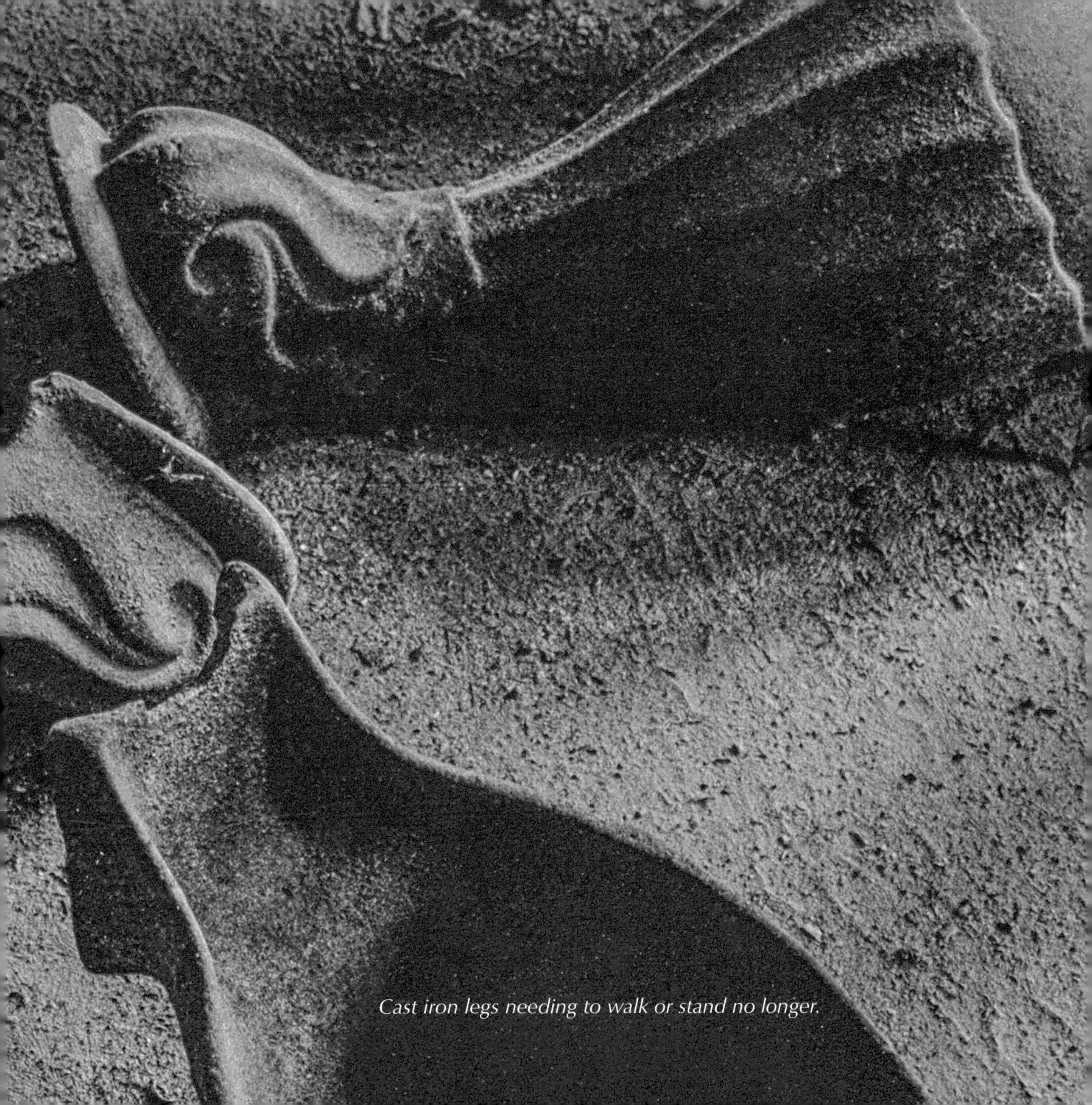

Cast iron legs needing to walk or stand no longer.

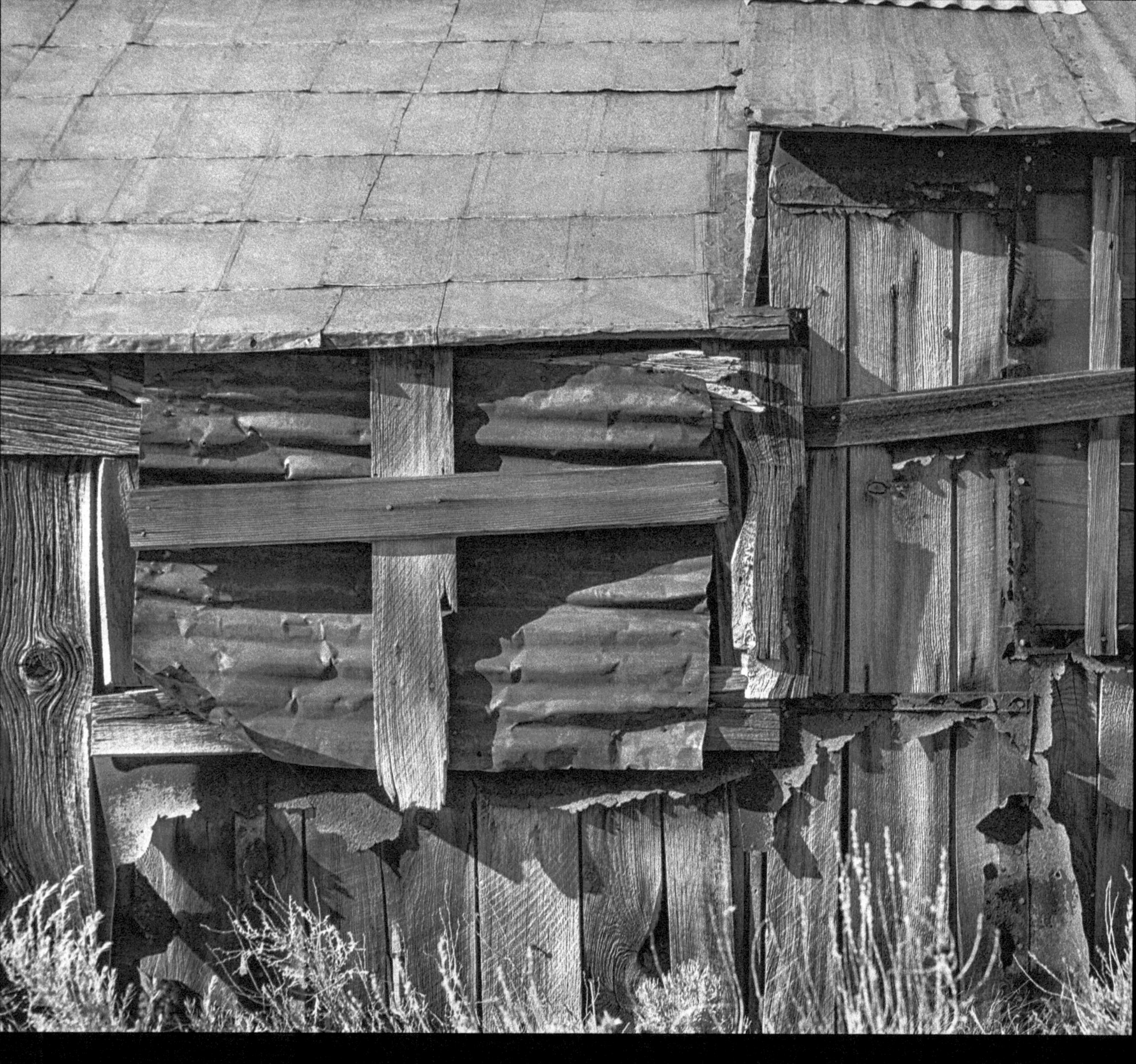

Keeping it all together, residents used whatever was at hand to fortify buildings against the elements. In the process, a serendipitous art form blossomed.

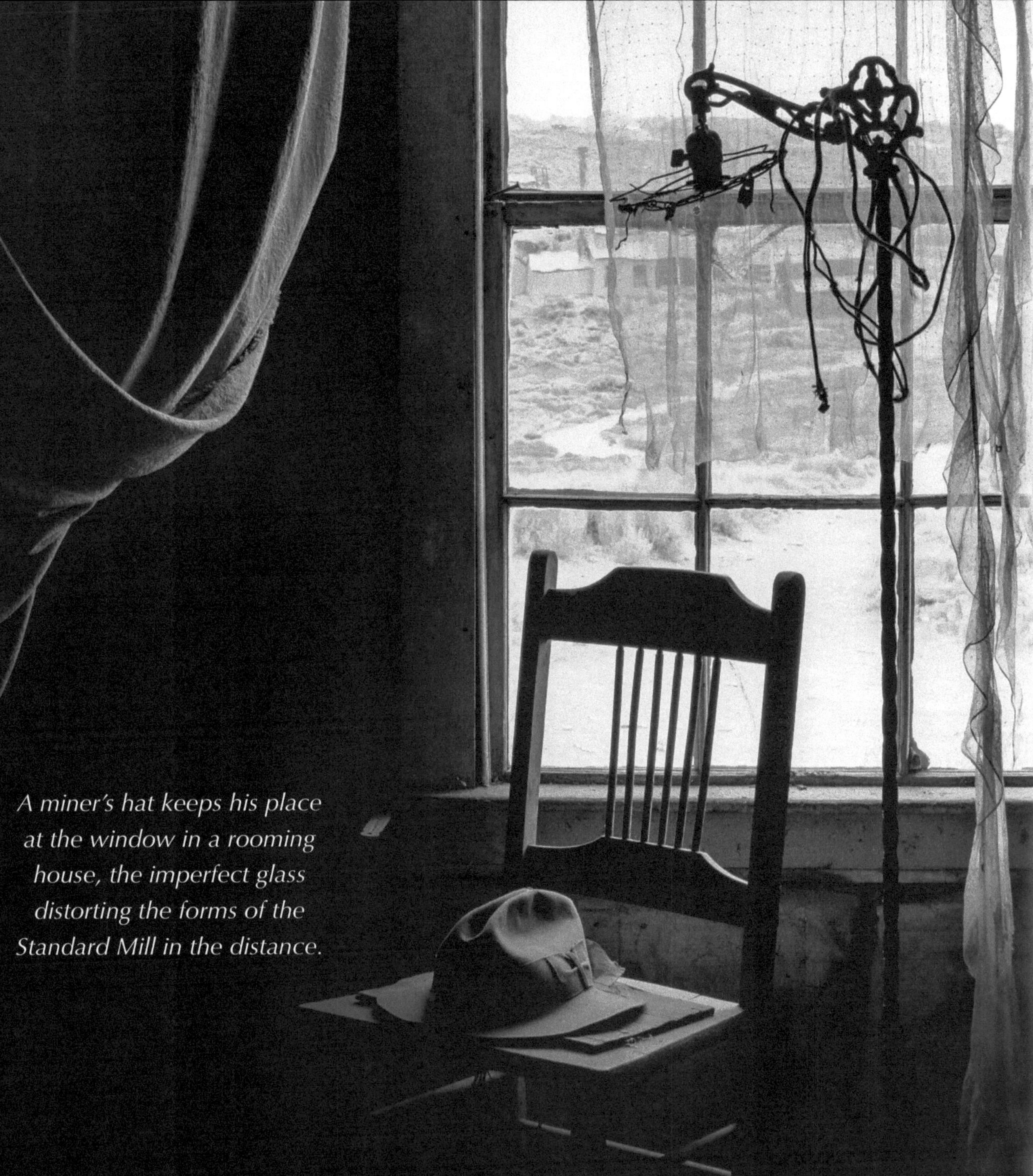

A miner's hat keeps his place at the window in a rooming house, the imperfect glass distorting the forms of the Standard Mill in the distance.

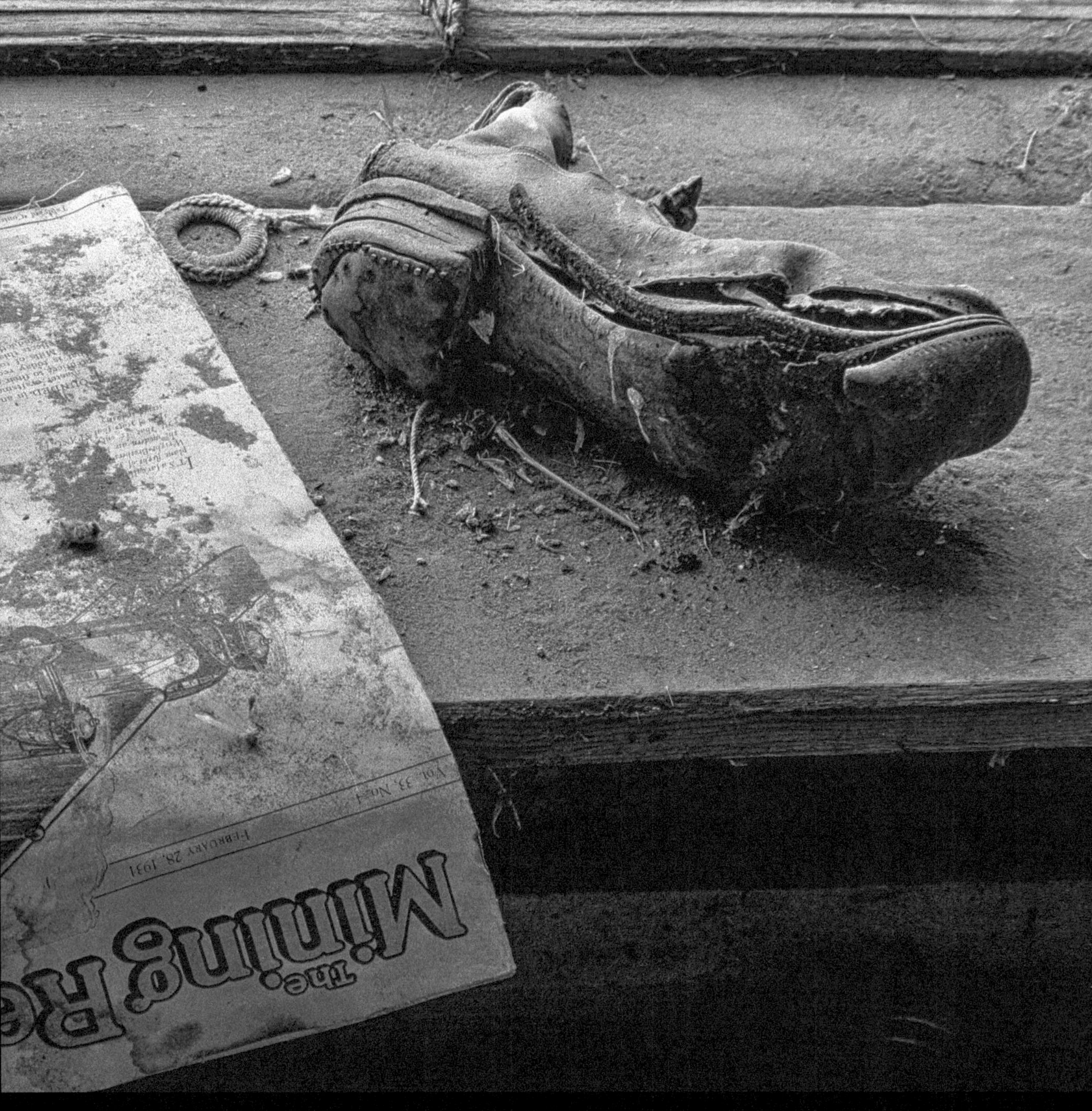

Having walked its last mile, this shoe assumes a state of repose on a workshop windowsill.

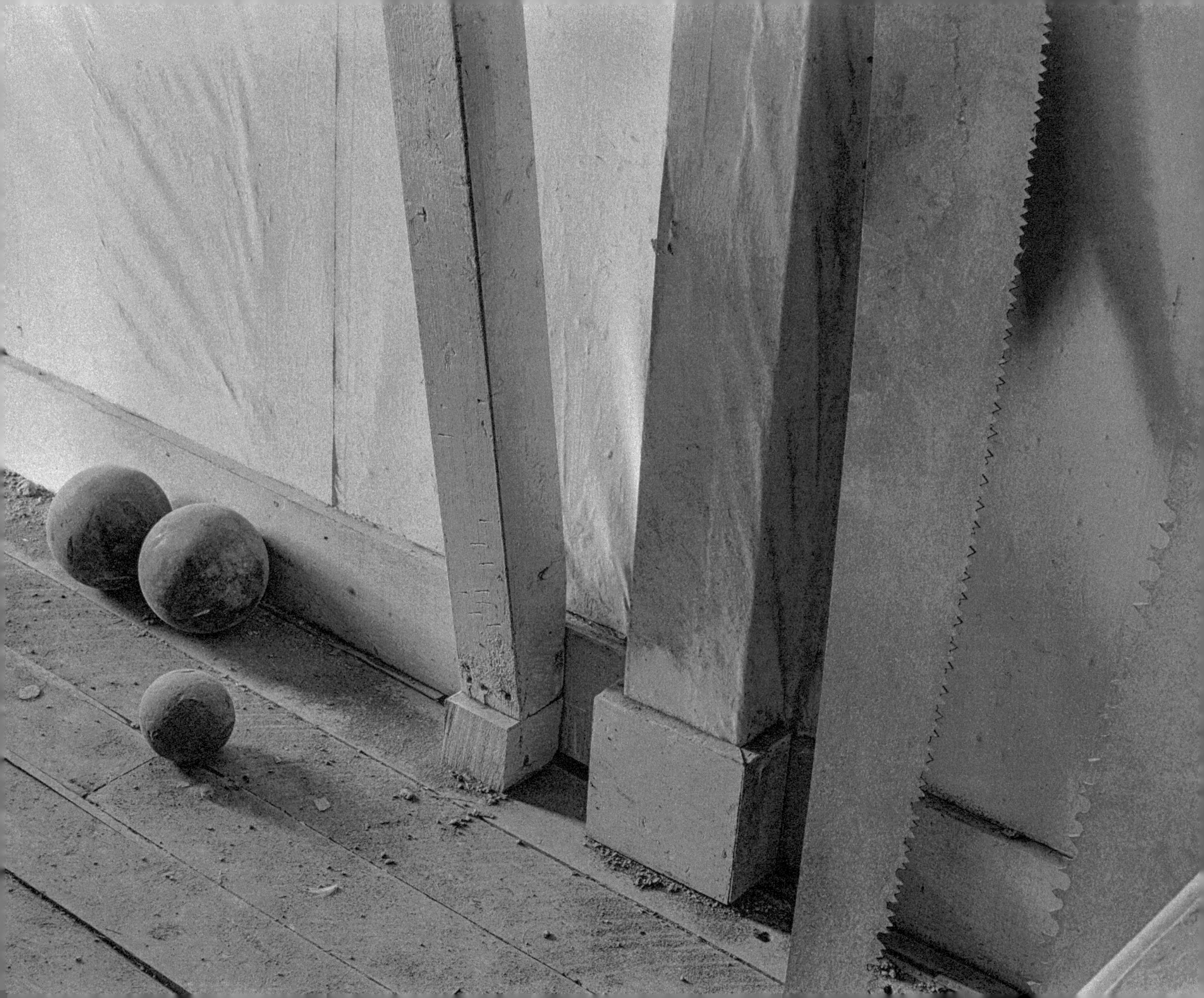

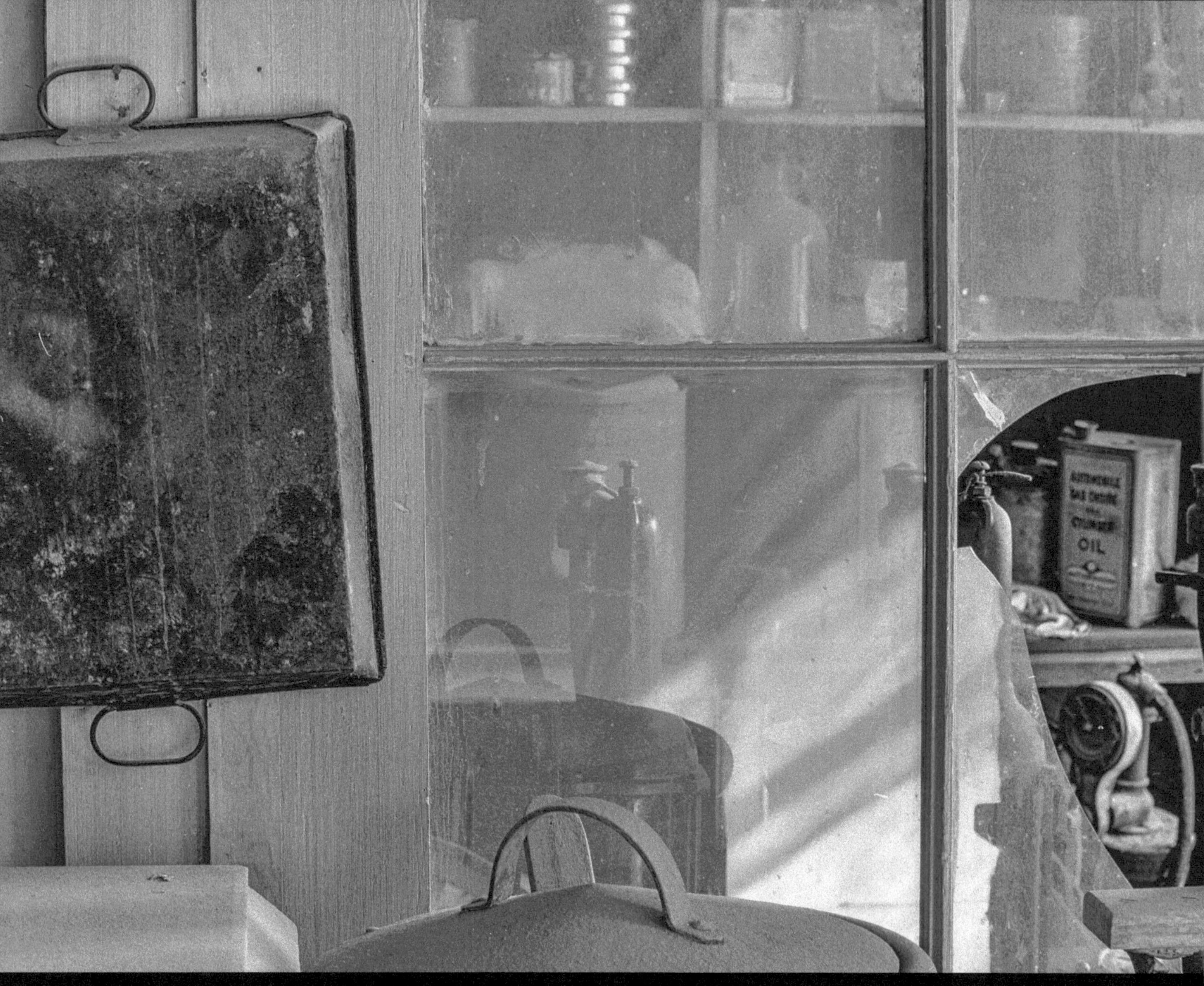

Dust, decay, and damage afford a wonderful modulation of light throughout the structures of Bodie. Silent to the ear, but a chorus to the eye.

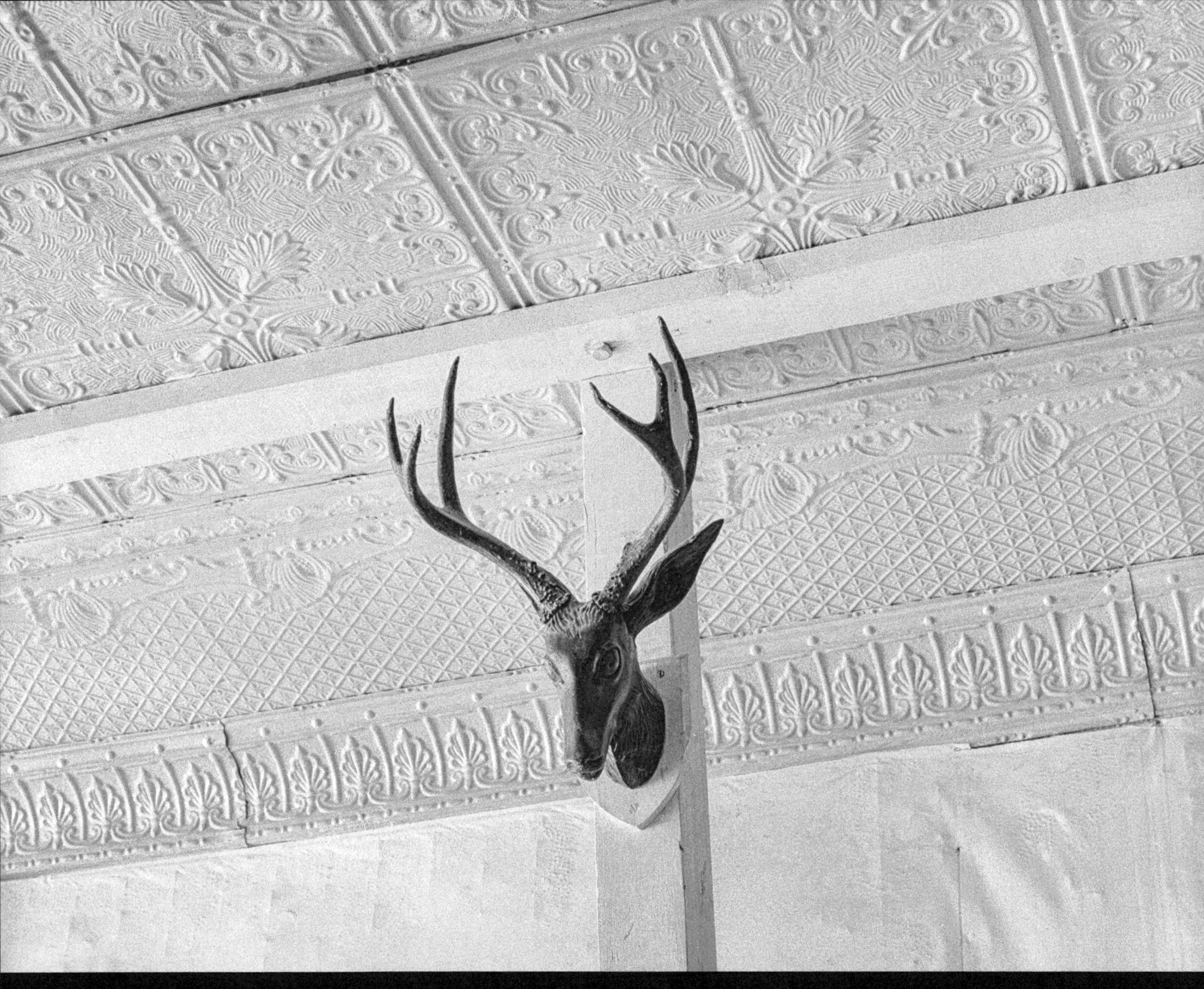

Looming from under a pressed tin ceiling, a stylized stag mocks the tradition of pool room taxidermy as it gazes over a billiard table.

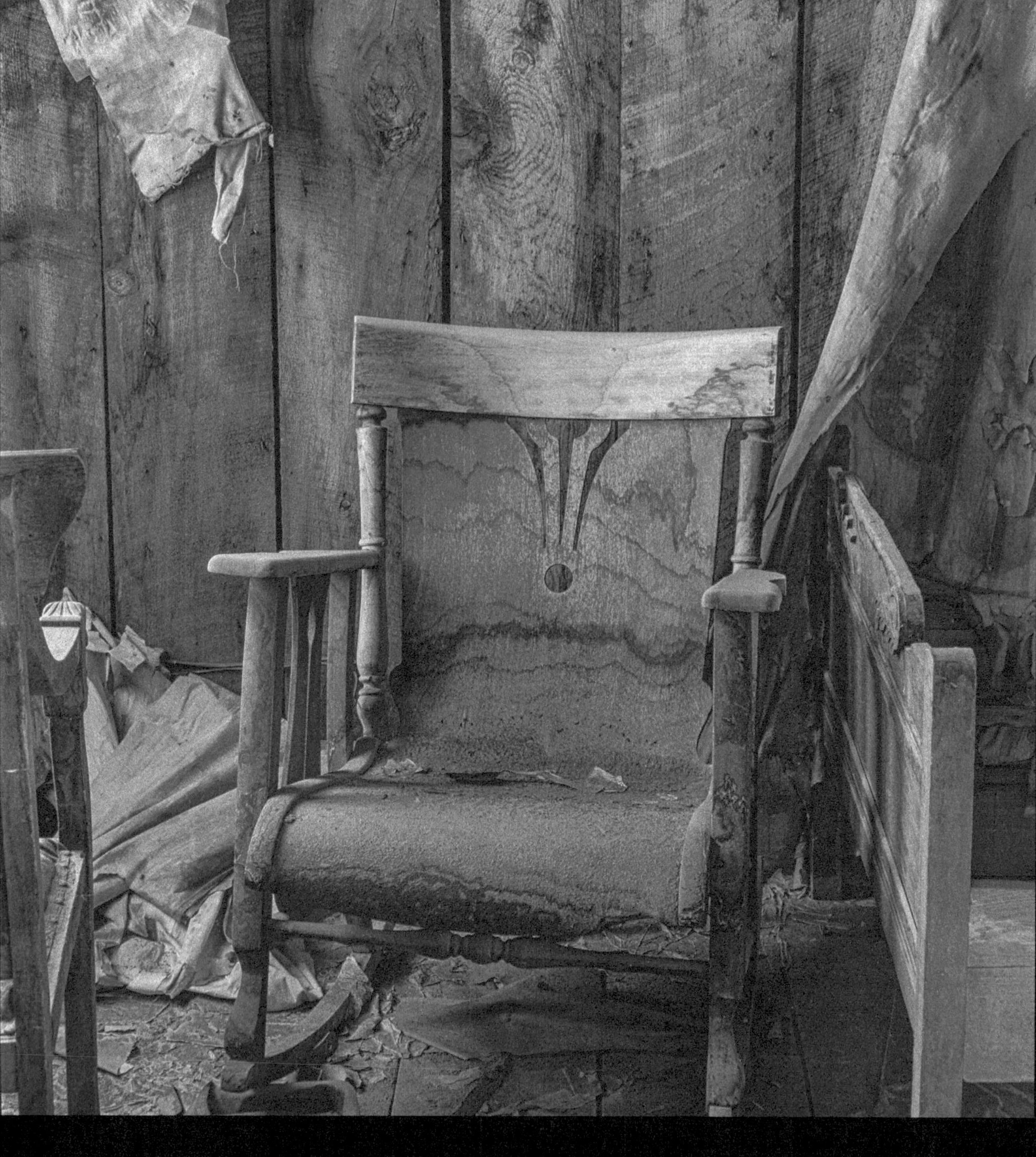

A chair sits in stasis, the potential for soothing its occupant still

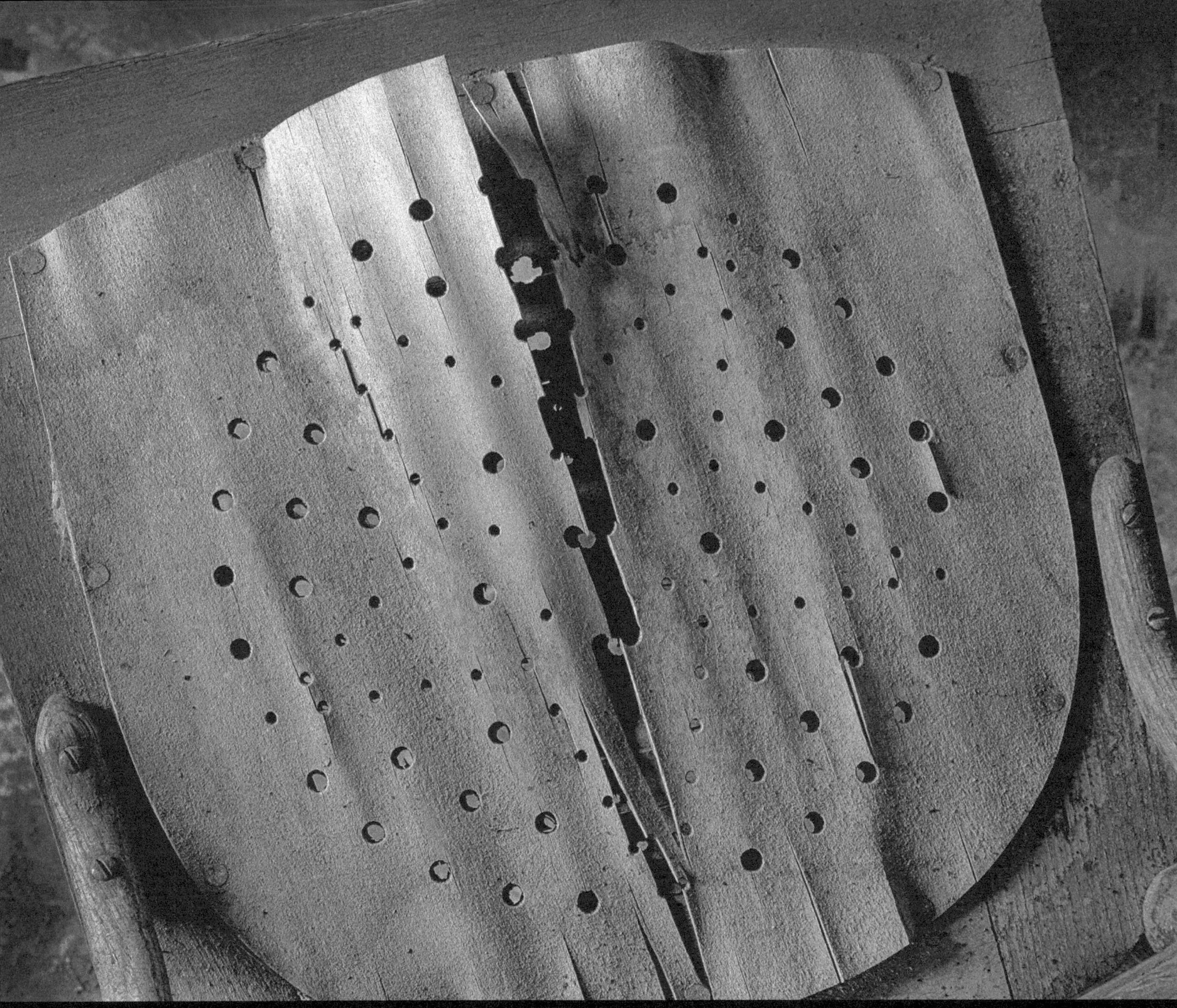

A perforated seat creates its own constellation, enriching the mythology of Bodie that continues today.

About the Author

Growing up in southern California, Pete Grady came to photography by way of drawing and painting. Cameras were around the house as he was growing up and that familiarity made using them a natural exercise. A valuable tool in support of his art as a visual notebook, eventually the photographs gained enough strength to become finished works on their own. Later when studying at university and and running low on funds, his fluency with photography proved valuable. He chanced into shooting live theater and found it to be a lucrative endeavor that expanded from there. While painting and drawing remained his passion, the practicalities of making a living were more easily served by photography and his career expanded, first into the technical fields of aerospace and the semiconductor industry, then transitioning into architectural, commercial, and business journalism. Pete lives in Boise, Idaho, with his wife, Joyce.

www.ingramcontent.com/pod-product-compliance
Lightning Source LLC
LaVergne TN
LVHW070224110826
845147LV00003B/640

9780976264217